I Love You Everywhere

VICTORIA K. HINDS

WESTBOW
PRESS®
A DIVISION OF THOMAS NELSON
& ZONDERVAN

WestBow Press books may be ordered through booksellers or by contacting:

WestBow Press
A Division of Thomas Nelson & Zondervan
1663 Liberty Drive
Bloomington, IN 47403
www.westbowpress.com
844-714-3454

ISBN: 978-1-6642-0500-0 (sc)
ISBN: 978-1-6642-0501-7 (e)

Library of Congress Control Number: 2020917395

Print information available on the last page.

WestBow Press rev. date: 10/20/2020

⇥ ♡ ⇤

I love your hands.
I love your feet.
I love your eyes and personality.

⇥ ♡ ⇤

‒≫ ♡ ≪‒

I love your forehead and your nose.
I love your mouth and
fingers and toes.

‒≫ ♡ ≪‒

⇢≫ ♡ ≪⇠

I love your stomach, chest, and hair.
I love you everywhere.

⇢≫ ♡ ≪⇠

⇥ ♡ ⇤

I love your style.
How you dare.
I love the tiger in your stare.

⇥ ♡ ⇤

‐→>> ♡ ‐<<‐

I love the laughter,
How you care.
I love you everywhere.

‐→>> ♡ ‐<<‐

➤ ♡ ◀

I love the love you give to me.
I love the way you love to be.
I love the way you make me breathe.

➤ ♡ ◀

—⟫— ♡ —⟪—

I love the passion underneath.
I love the love we share together—
How you ruffle all my feathers,
How you love so honestly.
I love the way
You cherish me.

—⟫— ♡ —⟪—

—≫ ♡ ≪—

I love the way you move and talk.
I love the way we take a walk.
I love the confidence we share

—≫ ♡ ≪—

⇉ ♡ ⇇

Every time we are together,
I love the knowledge in your head
And the way we say "amen."

⇉ ♡ ⇇

$\rightarrowtail \heartsuit \leftarrowtail$

I love the looks you give to me
When they're given tenderly.

$\rightarrowtail \heartsuit \leftarrowtail$

⇢⟫ ♡ ⟪⇠

I love the feeling in the air.
I love you everywhere.

⇢⟫ ♡ ⟪⇠

—≫ ♡ ≪—

I love it when we're under pressure.
When we're talking
about the weather.
When we're swinging on the porch,

—≫ ♡ ≪—

‚Äù‚û≠ ‚ô° ‚û≠‚Äú

And when we're gazing at the north.
I love watching you pull up
When you're coming
home from work.
I love the smell of your cologne
Whenever we're alone.

‚Äù‚û≠ ‚ô° ‚û≠‚Äú

–» ♡ «–

I love the way you do the slide
When you hear a song you like.
And when you're scooting next to me

–» ♡ «–

❧❤❧

And our legs touch suddenly.
I love the little things you do and
When you tell me "I love you."
I love you underneath the sun
And through all the
phases of the moon.

❧❤❧

⇢⇢ ♡ ⇠⇠

I love the smirks across the room
When I'm smirking at you too.
I love the airs you tend to make

⇢⇢ ♡ ⇠⇠

When a wink is all it takes.
I love the wrinkles on your face
And all the stories that you say.

—

-» ♡ «-

And everything you see as flaws
I do not see them at all.

-» ♡ «-

I love the little ways you care;
I love you everywhere.

⇥ ♡ ⇤

I love the way you sing me songs
When we're moving right along.
I love the jokes you love to tell me

⇥ ♡ ⇤

⇢⇢ ♡ ⇠⇠

When you think they're
kind of funny.
When you wear those ugly boots
And you switch to different shoes,

⇢⇢ ♡ ⇠⇠

➤➤ ♡ ◀◀

And when you tell me I look
lovely—doesn't matter what I do.
I always tell you what I think.
You're always showing me with truth.

➤➤ ♡ ◀◀

—≫ ♡ ≪—

I love the talents you possess
And all the ways you like to dress.
I love the collared shirts you wear

—≫ ♡ ≪—

$\rightarrow\!\!\!\succ \heartsuit \prec\!\!\!\leftarrow$

With just a T-shirt under there.
I love the way you take a bite and
When you let me talk all night.

$\rightarrow\!\!\!\succ \heartsuit \prec\!\!\!\leftarrow$

When you've poured yourself a cup,
But you end up giving it up.
I love the way you like to share
And the way we make a pair.

⇥ ♡ ⇤

I love how when we watch a movie
We end up playing footsy.
And the first thing that you do

⇥ ♡ ⇤

When I stand in front of you.
When you feel like playing tag,
And you want to win so bad.

--» ♡ «--

When we wake up in the morning,
And your eyes are hardly boring,
You tell me that I'm pretty,

--» ♡ «--

＊＊＊ ♡ ＊＊＊

And you take me to the city.
When we're sitting in the car
And we watch a shooting star;

＊＊＊ ♡ ＊＊＊

➤ ♡ ◀

And we say a little prayer.
I love you everywhere.

➤ ♡ ◀

⇥ ♡ ⇤

I love the way you say, "Let's go!"
Every time we watch a show.
When we talk about vacation

⇥ ♡ ⇤

⇻ ♡ ⇺

But decide that we are staying.
When you're whispering "goodnight"
And it's time to close our eyes.
And everything about the way
You like to hold me
through the night.

⇻ ♡ ⇺

❦

Thank you, Lord.
I'm feeling blessed.
Every moment is a gift.

❦

—>> ♡ <<—

When we don't know what to do,
I know we'll always do our best.
Father, help us through the toughness
And keep us in your hands.
Use us in a way that we're
supposed to understand.

—>> ♡ <<—

–»– ♡ –«–

And, to my darling:
See this ring,
We can get through anything.

–»– ♡ –«–

‑»‑♡‑«‑

I want to love you forever;
I want to give you what you need.
I know that sometimes
we can't do that,

‑»‑♡‑«‑

So let's get down on our knees
And remember all the
good times and
What those bad times had to teach.

—»— ♡ —«—

I love this peace and reassurance
And the way God made you speak.
And even if we don't like something,

—»— ♡ —«—

➤➤ ♡ ◄◄

I know He can help us see.
His voice is so commanding,
Like a calmness on the sea.
There's a wildness about it
That was made for you and me.

➤➤ ♡ ◄◄

—»> ♡ «—

I love you now and
I loved you then
And all the times that we begin.

—»> ♡ «—

＊≫ ♡ ≪＊

I love you here;
I love you there;
I love you everywhere.

＊≫ ♡ ≪＊

About the Author

Victoria Hinds is a God-fearing, half Hungarian, Midwestern native, who is also a loving wife, and a "Supermom" of six children. She holds a BA in Graphic Design from Upper Iowa University and an MBA in Marketing from University of Phoenix. After completing numerous studies, she used her skills as a Composition/Page Designer at The Geneseo Republic newspaper. In Texas at the Plano Star Courier and at Ad Pages Magazine, Victoria was able to enjoy being a Graphic Artist. Over the recent years, she has focused on taking care of her ever-growing family. The author's experiences have given her an overall unique perspective on life, which she has carried through in her poetry. Victoria's works serve as wonderful sources of inspiration that provide a sense of love, and compassion, and help readers stay connected and present with loved ones, and their surroundings--all to give God all the glory.

Printed in the United States
By Bookmasters